Between Worlds

A Poetry Book by

Be Budding

DEDICATION

To all who have loved me, encouraged me,
triggered me....

NAMASTE

I honor the place in you where the entire
Universe resides.

I honor the Light within you, because it is
also within me.

True understanding of Life is to turn inward
and love all the things that make you,
you.

These 44 poems floated to the surface
through the space of openness and
deepness.

A gift from me to you.

~ Be Budding

CONTENTS

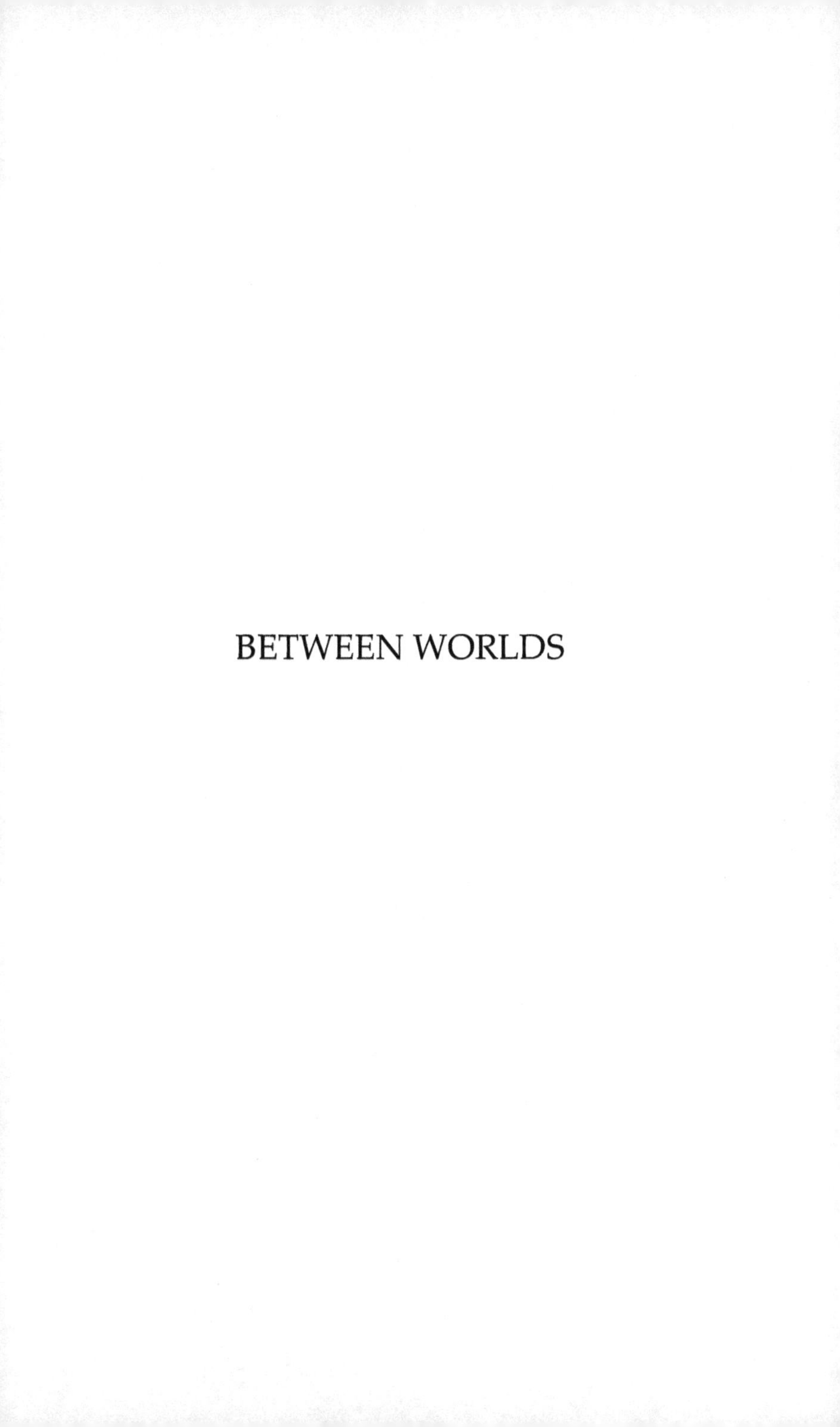

BETWEEN WORLDS

I felt like I was drifting Between Worlds

between the earth
and the moon
among the stars

in oceans and endless skies

what I just couldn't see was
that I was not far behind

I was in the right place
at the right time

here started my journey
to realign

seeking for the light
along the stem of the lotus flower

I regained my trust and power

the path of inner growth and transformation

I found my way through writing my deepest
pain and greatest joy on this piece of
paper.

DIVING DEEP

1. Budding Poetry

Words roll up the paper
Like a marble game
Tapping each other forward

To a higher level
A deeper meaning
A sense of being

A collaboration is born
Like waves becoming a sea
That is how poetry originates

Magically

A greater expression
A larger impression
Than each word separately

Creating a symphony
A composition of meaning
A living being

It is how life works
It is inviting you to play
You are the wave flowing

Naturally

As well as the sea
You are everywhere
And nowhere simultaneously

This is where I stay
This is the space between
This is where I am renewed

Over and over again
As an ongoing vibrancy
A higher frequency

I welcome you to my world of

Budding Poetry.

2. Calling

The Ocean is calling me,
endlessly

Can you hear the song
of the Sea?

The salt water
is whispering

Calling my name
"I want to swim with thee"

Please, dive deep
into the waves

Like you did as a child
when your soul was free

and ready to float
and be led by me

Yes, it's time
to dive deep

To surrender to the water
the source of life

Let me bring you home
be purified

Hear me
I am

The sweet song
of liberty

This is the invitation
the calling

Come home
swim with me.

3. Trust

Is the hardest thing to do
when you step into the unknown

Which way to go
left or right

Straight forward
and don't look behind

It's like stepping into the desert
without directions

Only the sun smiling at you
all day long

First it makes you mad
then you surrender

And follow its light in the sky
saying: you are close by

...

the next step in line

That's the way the Desert Rose
will unfold

Exposing the Promise
each one of the roses hold.

4. Rose Bud

Little Rose Bud
why do you cry

Dear little Rose Bud,
don't be shy

Why do you hide
your beautiful colors inside

Dear little beautiful Rose Bud
you behold so much more than you know

If you start to believe
you will grow

Stronger and bigger
empowered by the Light

It is such a wonderful sight
when you reflect your strength within

Dear little beautiful strong Rose Bud
there's no such thing as sin

Underneath your thick skin
there is only one thing

And as you gracefully unfold
you will show

Who you are and always have been
from the very start

The most precious flower I have ever seen

The Lover's Heart.

5. Choice

To flower or to wither
is a matter of Choice

The choice to open up
or to keep the door shut

You are not imprisoned
when you don't let yourself
fall down the slope

"There's something inside that they can't get
to,
that they can't touch. It's yours.
- Hope"

Looking through a kaleidoscope
I realize I choose the world I see

Quotes are no longer just words
I can feel them deep inside of me

All invisible shall live on and on
All physical in the end shall die

Choose happy thoughts in your mind
and it will give you wings to fly

Over the walls
of the prison you held

I think about Nelson Mandela, Edith Eger,
Viktor E. Frankl...
and how they must have felt

Great examples
of the power of thought

They have showed us the way
where liberation awaits

...

Forgiveness over Resentment
Love over Fear

An Anchor
I keep these words near

I repeat them in my mind
in the Hope I will find
the opening to a Meaningful Life

...

13

It is all about love not hate

From today
I hold on to my faith
I am thankful
for all I am
for all I have

For all that surrounds me

…

I look at the world as a place
with unlimited possibilities

Life is not ending
Life is beginning

Over and over again
It is a matter of choice

For me, that is the core,
the pathway to the life I adore

I am all in!

I wish you a magical ride

Promising
both you and me

The most beautiful Sunrise.

* Inspired by the movie 'The Shawshank Redemption'

6. Circle of Life

Remember, it's the Circle of Life
playing its game
doing what it does
just like bees buzz

Follow the flow
walk the way
fly like a butterfly flies
nature doesn't work in straight lines

Nothing is perfect
and then again
it is

In all its swirling
twisting and turning
you observe and see

That the process is always
processing

that is The Bliss.

7. The Beast

The Beast inside of me
that wants to tell me what to do

Grows bigger
if I let it rule

It wants to raise his voice
to my own mind

If I am not careful
it will make me blind

The Beast will make you small
The Beast will make you beg

But not if you stand tall
or better said, relax

Don't let yourself be beaten up
by the harsh voice inside

Turn your head and look up
to the bright sky

A Love for Life

Hear the bird's song
Hear the whispering of the wind

Softness
will settle in

You have all the time there is

No need to hurry
No need to rush

...

Grow slowly
little flower

Bigger and stronger

Time is on your side
as it always was.

SHOWING UP

8. White Flag

To fight or embrace
the shadow of the Light
To find or veil
the power buried inside

A deep dark hole
is inside every soul
No longer to ignore
it is part of us all, I'm sure

We hide our troubled stories in there
pretending they don't exist is not fair
Look into the depths of the Soul
it wants us to show

Black and white
is what forms the whole
Yin yang, the core of being
no censoring, but experiencing

Equal to each other
live side by side
Dark magic
will turn into Light

Instead of fighting
look yourself in the eye
Be brutally honest and know
there is no you and I

Who is without sin
cast the first stone
Peace starts within us
that is all we need to know

Like the sun we rise over water and land
to shine our light and expand
Our point of view
and see it clear

There has always been
a heart and spear
We live in a space of duality
but we decide our own reality

Penetrate, go deeper still,
until there is no more need to fulfill
Imagined limitations and expectations
this is how we find ease in our relations

And as the storm has died down
our home is found
Turning the unity consciousness
into a Bright Lightness

The world will sparkle and shine again
the Garden of Eden for women and men
We lay down our fist
finally, we're in the place where

...

23

Unconditional Love exists.

9. Show your face

This is what I heard
the last few days
'Show your face'

In the midst of the night
I like to fight
the bitterness

I feel alone
and scared

I don't know who I am
'What is my plan?'

I don't like to surrender
I feel so vulnerable

I don't want to fall apart
and show my weak heart

25

But what when you can't go on
holding on to what you used to know

What if the true story wants to show?

There is no other way,
you must show up
put down your warrior face

Surrender to Love.

10. Breathe

I breathe life
I breathe sunlight

I breathe flesh
I breathe bones

I breathe experience
I breathe goddess

I breathe

I breathe air
I breathe water

I breathe the ocean
I breathe the sea

I breathe the fog
I breathe the sky

I breathe the clouds
Passing by

I breathe history
I breathe future

I breathe you
I breathe me

I breathe the soil
That anchors me

I stand my ground
As strong as I can

I am

A flower of wisdom
Firm and elegant

...

I am Life

I shine
I bend

…

Always doing the best I can.

11. Narrow Window

A heavy day
explodes in my view

Full, no space behind
my endless speaking mind

I want to hear
I want to fly

Underneath the wings
of the Earth less needing sky

No gravity
holding me down

Just let
all stories be drown

Setting free
of my imaginary truth

...

As I learned in my youth

Relaxing
Letting all anxiety go

Breathe in Breathe out
Flow

Outside of that Narrow Window.

12. White Rose

White Rose
soft and sweet
I am incomplete

White Rose
passing by
'Which word is mine?'

White Rose
why are you here
'To show me your gentle tear?'

Your touch
Your smile
is like a mirror in which I see mine

I look deep in my eyes
and find myself drifting
between the ice

It is cold
as I am passing by
the sharp edges of Life

They cut me like a knife
I survive
and emerge

Through the White Rose's eye

I arise
in the breeze
and take flight

Hair blowing
with sparkling eyes
wide open

I come to Light.

13. Time Traveler

Layer through layer
I go

Down down
the Everglow

Through the Earthly Sky
I dive

Till I find
my soul connection

Taking flight

Layer through layer
I go

Down down
the Everglow

To expose what is
hidden inside

Wanting to be discovered
and start to shine

Layer through layer
I go

Down down
the Everglow

Waiting to put
my feet on the ground

Where my actions show
what I am really about

Layer through layer
I go

Down down
the Everglow

To put Heaven
on Earth

Right here
I find my Re-birth

Layer through layer
I go

Down down
the Everglow

Deeper and deeper
'till I find

There is only one thing left
budding inside

Layer through layer
I go

Down down
the Everglow

I don't need to be
high in the Sky

Right here on Earth
my soul revives

Down down
I go

Finding peace
inside Everyday Life.

* Inspired by the music of Coldplay

14. Mind, Body and Soul

Who do you let be
the head of your masterpiece

Who is in charge
of this three-dimensional
triangle

Have you put your dots
and drawn a line?

'Cause, when you
connect them all

You will find

The great power hidden behind
this magical pentagram

A Universal Masterplan

...

A passage occurs
to the Union of Three

A Great Force of Energy

Like a pearly soap bubble
you will float through the air

Never scared
always true

...

Knowing…

this hidden power is within you.

GROWING UP

15. The Frog

Would you recognize
the Frog Prince
if you meet him

Would you kneel down
to look him straight
in the eye

Knowing
he is your savior
in disguise

Look behind
appearances
and let him live
inside your house

Then,
in the shadows
of the well

43

You can't tell
him from your own

And by that
he will be crowned
as the prince that he is

Emerging
your Golden Ball
showing you are

the Greatest Love of All.

16. Own your Throne

You and you
alone
can be on your
throne

Listen to the
voice
of your dear
heart

It is telling you your path
It shows
the signs on
the road

Guiding you back home

...

45

Come, and claim your throne!

17. Soul's Purity

I have searched
for my soul

In the deepest depths
of my bones

Who am I?
What will I become?
What is my song?

What does the world
show
reflect back to me?

Where is my sanity?

What is the purpose
of the whole?

Where is my home?

I dream
and drift away

Thinking:
'Where is my place?'

Finding
at the end of the stream

The root
of all beginnings

I enter the gate
through dimensions
fantasy, illusionary

I am
in the midst of the bubble

Where is no struggle
only

…

The Blue Lagoon
The Colorful Meadow

The Source from which everything grows

Here is no need, just me
Here is no noise, just silence
Here is no rush, just be

...

49

A Resurrection of Soul's Purity.

18. Rabbit Hole

The ultimate test…

Can we rise above the polarities
of what is true and what is fantasy

Can we see each other as perfect and whole
even when we go down another Rabbit Hole

Can we find each other inside the cave
a dark muddy warm loving birthing place

Can we relax and see
a possibility for a New Way to be

Can we care about each other
and Mother Earth

Can we see, there always will be an end
and a new birth

Can we see that this is not about us
'cause our bodies will eventually perish
and turn to dust

Can we see it is about the peace we hold
and that this is the perfect opportunity
for that to unfold

Yes, can we meet deep down
in the cave of the same Rabbit Hole?

Hold each other close because we know
we will rise above and pass the test

If it is

True Love

that we will show.

19. Time

We often live in Chronos time
Living by the clock

We try to capture the moment
but it gets stuck

Hidden behind our phones
we cannot experience
what the picture really beholds

Life wants us to feel
another way of time

Events between you and me
A life lived through children's eyes

Kairos time,
moment for moment
for you to see

That your camera is in your heart
The space where all memories start

That's the key

Choose Kairos
and the illusion will no longer be

Time bends
making you remember
every single life event

The beauty of this contradiction
is in the openness between the attachments

The truth of the reality
is that time is just a fantasy

Get loose, open up
and you'll be freed
from the Hands of the Clock.

20. Is

'Who am I?'
An idealist or a realist

Actually, both don't exist
It's a story we tell
ourselves

What is the comparison
between these two opposites

Of is is,
because is is, and is, is not, not is

Do you know this?
There is and there is not is

That means that an idealist or a realist
does not exist

And because it does not exist
It exists

In our minds
They are stories we tell ourselves

You are the one or the other
but that is never the case

Because without the realist
the idealist does not exist
and vice versa

And because both can't exist
without the other

The conclusion is
there is only
Is

In this Is, we Exist

One time you act like an idealist
The other time like a realist

What is the one without the other?
Without the idealist the realist
does not dream

Without the realist
the idealist is
never able to make a difference

No, one can't exist
without
the other

And therefore there is
only one that exists

And that is

...

57

Is.

21. Treasures

When you turn
your world upside down
inside out
treasures
will be found

When you walk
off the beaten path
life unfolds
the book
you have

Your story
buried deep inside
reveals itself
behind each curve
of this magical wonder ride

Life is meant
to fall in love
with the sun
and its beautiful colors
up above

Lifeforce is blowing
wanting us to inhale
to receive and expand
to connect
and tell our tale

Exhibit the story
for others to be seen
as an example of
how life could be
when you turn the key

...

Magic appears
like finding little blue feathers
under a tree

The moment you embrace
what was already given

to you and me.

61

RISING UP

22. Tree Power

Stand tall

Be as proud as a Tree

Respect your roots
A tribute to history

Follow your branches too
as they reach out to the world

Growing into endless possibilities
of life's Mysteries

Feel the budding leaves
when they open up and flower

A symbol of

...

the Manifestation of your Hidden Inner
Power.

23. I am love

Today I picked a card
'I am Love'

The card is about
facing my pain

Pain of not being seen
'There is no one to blame'

Is what I hear
What does that mean?
Don't I count?

'You don't need to be loud
to be heard
in the wilderness of sound

You're magic
precisely as you are

You are a gift to the Universe

Between Worlds

You only have to remember your worth

Keep strong in your belief
and you shall see

That what you desire
is already on its way

To manifest itself
into your reality

As little birds have
the most beautiful song

There is nothing wrong
All is right

Give up your fight
You can live with ease

'Cause you are love
and that is all God sees. '

24. One

The time of struggle
is passing by
We have to work together
look each other
in the eye

You're beautiful
yes, it's true

It is time for
one-ness

For me and you

"Give me One,
'Cause One is the best
In Confusion,
Confidence"

. . .

Give me Peace
A Mind of Trust

My Desire is to Be

One, with all the Rest of Us.

* Inspired by the music of Coldplay

25. Gold

Life is a Gift
so you can explore

What you want to feel,
touch and adore

At this horizon
where you are

You can shimmer and shine
or decline

You choose
what to do

But when you want to flourish
you have to sow what will bloom

Your seeds want to grow
Flowers will show themselves soon

Have faith
be patient and follow
your talents
your peace of mind
and you will find
the space
where alchemy takes place

This Universal Law is the heartbeat

The energy
from which all Life begins

Look inside your heart
your treasure is found within

Make a start
no matter how big or small

...

Success is Guaranteed
Sparkle you Shall

You have a Promise you Hold
Find your Pieces of Gold

Brush them Up
Make them Glow

They will Become
Bigger and more Bright

...

Spreading…

Golden Flashes of Magical Starlight.

26. Bridges

Build a bridge
if you want to grow

Build a bridge
and let the waters flow

From the mountaintop
to the open sea

Reach from heart to heart
and set your inner child free

A child that wants to play
and be amazed

Show her the world
don't be afraid

Build a bridge
tell your tale

...

73

Believe, and you shall not fail

Find the Bridge
Look above and beyond

And you will receive

All the Wonders of Love.

27. Heavenly Song

What do you see?

Do you see a heart that is broken
or do you see pieces of the heart
finding their way back home?

Do you see a shattering
or do you see a gathering

A connection through the heart
or a falling apart

What do you believe
What is your faith

Oneness or separation
You have your say

Are you already home
or are you flying around

In the center of the whole
or do you wander about

Do you feel the pull
of the great Galactic Center

Do you want to enter
or do you decide otherwise

There is no wrong
or right

Just listen
to the whisper

Carrying you to the next level
in the composition
of the Heavenly Song

You will find your place

...

76

The Heart where you Belong.

28. Stars

In these times
it is necessary
to take care of
ourselves
more than ever

To stand our
ground
peacefully
and joyfully
together

The illusion
tells us
we are separated
from our soul
our inner truth

Today,
we are ready
to open up
to our beliefs
to ourselves

We are not separate
We are whole
We are not egocentric
We are perfect souls

We are not lost, we are found

Like Endless Stars
Never Bound

Free we float
Across dimensions, over rainbows

…

79

We are Here and There
We are Everywhere

Free as One
We rise

In the Light of the Everlasting Sun.

OPENING UP

29. Golden Pages

Turn your life
into Pages of Gold

Write your story
it will unfold
who you are meant to be

a Writer in its Sanctity

Word by word
Step by step

You follow your
self into
the depth
of the sky

A place where
sparkles
lighten up
the air

You fly

Like confetti
falling
down
one's hair

Like a flamingo
that walks on by

Your feet will
dance

Your eyes will
smile

Your hands will
create

Your Tribute to Life

...

You will
Find your Way
And fly
Far, Far away

Like a Pigeon

With wings
of Golden Pages

...

85

A Story told throughout the Ages.

30. I am

I am a reader and a writer
A mother and a daughter
I am here and there
In heaven and on earth

I am a body and a soul
A do-er and a thinker
An extrovert and introvert
I am life giving birth

I am mad and sad
I am love and loved
I am jolly and at ease
I do what I like and never cease

I don't need and I want
I take care and ask without apology
I give and receive
In all I do I am completely me

I create and I sleep
I knit and I write poetry
I laugh and I cry
And whenever I like, I say goodbye

I am not one thing
I am all at once
I am energy, electric, pulsing
Creativity, bursting from my Soul's Energy

I follow my path and stand still when I like
I look inside and outside
I am Between Worlds, left and right
Abundancy is what I find

I am nothing and everything
Source and a Human Being
I am circular and everlasting
A never ending story, always manifesting

...

I am Powerful and Weak
Vulnerable and Strong like a Heartbeat
I am the Future and the Past
I am in the Moment and Free at Last.

31. It is Time

To realize
more and more
which energy
is yours
and which
is not

When you sense
the stress
in your body
slow down
surrender
to explore

That feeling
within
be open
to receive
the gift
of clairsentience

Soon enough
you begin
to notice
what
you feel
is yours or not

It can be
lower energy
trying to
pull you
down
a bit

Don't judge it
instead be
compassionate
to the soul
expressing
a wound

While you are
in the knowing
this pain
is not yours
so you can
let go of it soon

And as
you do
it is like
a balloon
released from
your grip

The energy
can travel
lightly again
as you are not
meant to
hold it

The only way
is up
for you
to go
and we
are so happy

Now you
know
you can release
anything
you like
without storing

It in your
being
it is not necessary
to bind
pain
in materiality

If you want
you can
let go
of what was
never yours
to start with

We want you
to remember
your only
way
is up
indeed

And as you
see
the pain
and tears
disappear
in the ocean

…

The Endless Sea

Back to

Source Energy

Back To

Life

That is the way you'll

Survive

...

95

To be who you really are
Let nothing and nobody hold you down

The Only Way is up

Let's work on that from now.

32. Wonderland

I wonder
the meaning of existing

Then I hear
a subtle voice within, saying:

Don't overthink
follow the stream

The joy of your heart
and you will see

Like Alice in Wonderland
that the world bends
when you don't interfere
Just follow the road you are sent

You will be surprised
as you find

Magic is everywhere
it is the Source of Life

Keep believing
hold your faith

Don't let go
to your time and space

In your own little world
where fantasy lives

Miracles happen
You just have to believe this

Know this, feel this
in every cell and bone

Follow what you know
Wisdom will guide you home

Just like Alice

You are the writer of your story
The dreamer of your dream

You will thrive
for empowerment is yours

You are your own
energy giving Life Force

You will find your bliss
Your beautiful inner garden

Dig, weed, seed,
give water

To your flowers
and your world will grow

...

Just as Alice
You will open your eyes

And see
Life is just what you believe

Mirroring your fantasy
While you are sitting

Save and peacefully
Underneath the life tree

Believe me
You cannot not survive

...

It is an Universal Law

Just Explore

This is
The Way of Life.

33. Put your hands in my hands

Put your hands in my hands
No need to control
Together we float
Over seas, in stormy weather, over the
meadow

Put your hands in my hands
Here you can see
You are loved and cared for
A river running free

Put your hands in my hands
I see the Light in you
Shining just like me
We are the same

Both sitting at the foot of the

- Forever Life-giving Tree -

Put your hands in my hands
Let me bring you home
Earth is the place you live
Heaven where your soul is always whole

Put your hands in my hands
And sit together
Under this gorgeous tree
Feel the inner peace and harmony

Put your hands in my hands
I will never let you go
You can't fall off
I am the wind, the spreading bee

The force of life, setting you free

I will reach for you
Where ever you are
Just put your hands in my hands
Surrender, and we will travel far

Over the rainbow
To worlds yet unseen
With your crown in the sky
Your feet in the mud

You will grow forever

...

Like a Flower, you will Bud.

34. Acceptance

Acceptance is love
Love is acceptance
Acceptance of yourself
Acceptance of another

Acceptance of Love
as Whole

Can you loosen the strings
Untie the knot

Can you walk barefoot
in total freedom

Can you let go
of all of your expectations

And let love
spin in the air

Freewheeling
Dazzling

Not to be caught
or held firm

But to be shared,
admired
and cherished

If you let this be

The Acceptance of Love
will
set you
totally and completely

Free.

35. Truth

The Truth is
you are all free

You are NOT alone, small,
angry, pathetic

YOU are all
you need

The moment you remember
the truth

Is the moment
you won't hold grief

No more asking,
wanting, pushing

No more offering,
pleasing, telling

...

Only living in the Knowing
That Freedom is yours

Joined in this Inner Peace
You swim out to Open Sea

Back to Source.

36. Two Pearls

God told her
You are two pearls
in one oyster

They had time to grow
buried deeply in your
heart and soul

Now they are whole
and it is time
for you to let them show

Your beautiful
aqua colored
shiny stones

They are given to you
not to hide
but to wear them
with dignity and pride

Open your oyster
for people to see
the beauty inside
your hidden sea

Glitter and shine
you'll do fine

In the outside world

where I'll be yours
and you'll be mine

A re-connection in the Light
Of the forever Sunshine.

37. Ultimate Goal

When you do nothing
nothing is exactly
what is going to happen

What do you want your life to be?
What do you dream?

Everything is in your hands
as life presents
endless opportunities

On each corner that you cross
Every crossroad that you pass

There is a chance
A choice given
To live or die

Don't worry
it will not fly by

Life is never ending
Always yours
Never lost

You can't fall off

So try, experience and feel
what do you want to be real?

What do you want from life?

Turn the wheel
Choose your course

No matter where you are
What your circumstances may be
You can always return to source

Many people before us
have taught and shown
in your mind you are always Free

Choose your Reality
In every Moment

Every step along the Way
Choose the Path you want to take

Don't blame others
Take ownership
Of your Mind, Body and Soul

That is the Ultimate Life-Goal.

LIGHTENING UP

38. Over the Rainbow

The balloon is up
and can't
be stopped
as the rainbow
opens each heart

Showing a new doorway
to the gloriousness
of humanity

Step all in
to see what's behind
the dark blinds

Endless possibilities
is what you'll find

Are you willing
to step in
let go
and show
the deepest of your soul

To become aware
that behind the scene
there is only light

True majesty in Bright Sunlight.

39. Home Base

The Sun arises
in the East

He opens the door
and shines his
light in me

Showing
I am the child
of God

Holding me
in this graceful space
called Earth

My Home Base.

40. What wants me, will come to me

What wants me,
I want
and what I want,
wants me

It will come
like a happy dog

Running free

With ears
fluttering in the wind

And a smile
on its face

Never bound
by time and space

Playful it comes
my way

Like it wants to say:

'Did you call my name?'

Nor like a master
Nor as a student

But as two electrons
becoming an union

Two friends
happy to be
in each other
companionship

Both enjoying
the walk
no strings
attached

Just a perfect match

We acknowledge
each other as
part of the talk

Together
on adventure

Together
alone

And in that
relinquishment

we return Home.

41. White Feather

White feather
What is your message for me?
The message is:

'You are so much more
than you ever thought
you could be

There is a big truth
inside of you
you know

A Voice
A Calling
A Glow

Wanting to say:
Look deep inside
there is your doorway

At first you will not see
as you focus on the darkness
and not on me

But once you relax
you'll be amazed
by all the twinkling stars

A thousand Angels
dancing
in the Sky

One of them left me behind
to remind you
of your Inner Sight

Put on your wings and fly
through the nightfall
into the sunlight'

...

Where you lit a candle
In your own core
Creating a big power store

Entering a new space
And from the blindness
You are free

Never more in disguise
But always in the Light
Where you forever will

...

123

Be.

42. Love

I am in love
I am so happy
I am Love

I feel
I hear
I see

Sunbeams entering

My heart
My soul
My life

All cells
of my skin
respond
to the echo
inside

My teeth
whiter
than before
reveal a smile
I can't ignore

My hair
thicker, stronger,
waving more and more
as I enter the
dance floor

Sparkles of Light surround me

I feel them
I hear them
I see them
I touch them
I sing them
I dance them

...

I face the Truth
I am in Love
with Life itself

It is clear
no more hiding
or disguising

...

127

Love is here.

43. Blessed

I feel BLESSED
By Nature
By Gaia
By Universe

I feel BLESSED
By God
By Love
By Sunshine

I feel BLESSED

Through the clouds
shines a light
That sparkles in my eyes

I feel LOVED

...

And through
this Shimmering Light
I see

A Glimpse
of the Universe
inside of
me

A Reflection of Soul's Clarity.

44. As the Sun Arose

As I walked out the door
This morning
I could hear
The world sing

The notes of
The birds' songs
Floated through the air
Like snowflakes

Falling down
On me
Softly touching
My skin

Reaching my ear
Where they
Peacefully entered
My world within

I walked on
And saw the dew
On the meadows
As the Sun Arose

A rooster crowed
In the distance
And the only thing
I could think of was

That this world is
As a bright star
Shining her light
In disguise

When you hear it
You see it
When you see it
You hear it

...

Open up
Your senses
And you will know
This world is

Just perfect.

A RENEWED WORLD

Entering a Renewed World

This is not the End,
but a New Beginning.

About the author

Be Budding is the pen name of the author.
She chose this name because 'budding' means
the opening of a flower or showing signs of a
promise in a particular sphere.

In 2019 she went on an inner journey to
reconnect with her true self and started writing.

This poetry book is the creative expression of
that journey and is the reflection of her own
transformation from an administrative assistant
into an intuitive writer.

She hopes these poems will inspire you to
explore yourself. To never give up on the magic
of life. Instead surrender to your inner cravings,
over and over again.

Find a way to express your soul and be that gift
to the world you were always meant to be.

ENHANCE YOUR EXPERIENCE

You are invited to expand your experience with the *Between Worlds Workbook* or the *Between Worlds Card Deck*.

Visit:
bebudding.com to order the companion workbook and carddeck. Let this be your sanctuary for reflection, healing, and growth as you travel between worlds.

If you'd like to share insights you've gained, please leave a review on *Amazon* or share a picture of the book with a few words on *Instagram* & tag @be_budding.

For the other books in the *Worlds Series* visit:

bebudding.com

ISBN: 978-90-831988-0-4

Copy editing by Christian Belz
Cover design by Islam Farid

9 789083 198804